Iowa

Julie Murray

Big Buddy BOOKS

Explore the United States

VISIT US AT
www.abdopublishing.com

Published by ABDO Publishing Company, PO Box 398166, Minneapolis, MN 55439.

Printed in the United States of America, North Mankato, Minnesota.
032012
092012

 PRINTED ON RECYCLED PAPER

Coordinating Series Editor: Rochelle Baltzer
Editor: Sarah Tieck
Contributing Editors: Megan M. Gunderson, BreAnn Rumsch, Marcia Zappa
Graphic Design: Adam Craven
Cover Photograph: *iStockphoto*: ©iStockphoto.com/markmortensen.
Interior Photographs/Illustrations: *Alamy*: Clint Farlinger (p. 17), Lyroky (p. 27), Philip Scalia (p. 11); *AP Photo*: AP Photo (p. 25), Hoover Library (p. 23), Linda Kahlbaugh (p. 26), Charlie Neibergall (p. 27), North Wind Picture Archives via AP Images (p. 13), Telegraph Herald, Jessica Reilly (p. 26); *Getty Images*: Jonathan Daniel (p. 21), Norm Thomas/Photo Researchers (p. 30); *Glow Images*: Joseph Sohm (p. 23), Tom Till (p. 29); *iStockphoto*: ©iStockphoto.com/impactimage (p. 9), ©iStockphoto.com/SMWalker (p. 5), ©iStockphoto.com/SWKrullimaging (p. 27); *Shutterstock*: Walter G Arce (p. 9), Steve Byland (p. 30), Phillip Lange (p. 30), oksana2010 (p. 30), riddlerr (p. 19).

All population figures taken from the 2010 US census.

Library of Congress Cataloging-in-Publication Data

Murray, Julie, 1969-
Iowa / Julie Murray.
    p. cm. -- (Explore the United States)
ISBN 978-1-61783-353-3
1. Iowa--Juvenile literature. I. Title.
F621.3.M875 2012
977.7--dc23
                                    2012000757

Contents

ONE NATION

The United States is a **diverse** country. It has farmland, cities, coasts, and mountains. Its people come from many different backgrounds. And, its history covers more than 200 years.

Today the country includes 50 states. Iowa is one of these states. Let's learn more about Iowa and its story!

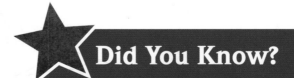

Did You Know?

Iowa became a state on December 28, 1846. It was the twenty-ninth state to join the nation.

Iowa's covered bridges are famous. They were featured in books and a movie.

Iowa Up Close

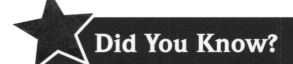

Did You Know?

Washington DC is the US capital city. Puerto Rico is a US commonwealth. This means it is governed by its own people.

The United States has four main **regions**. Iowa is in the Midwest.

Iowa shares borders with six states. Minnesota is north. Wisconsin and Illinois are east. Missouri is south. Nebraska and South Dakota are west.

Iowa has a total area of 56,273 square miles (145,746 sq km). More than 3 million people live in the state.

REGIONS OF THE UNITED STATES

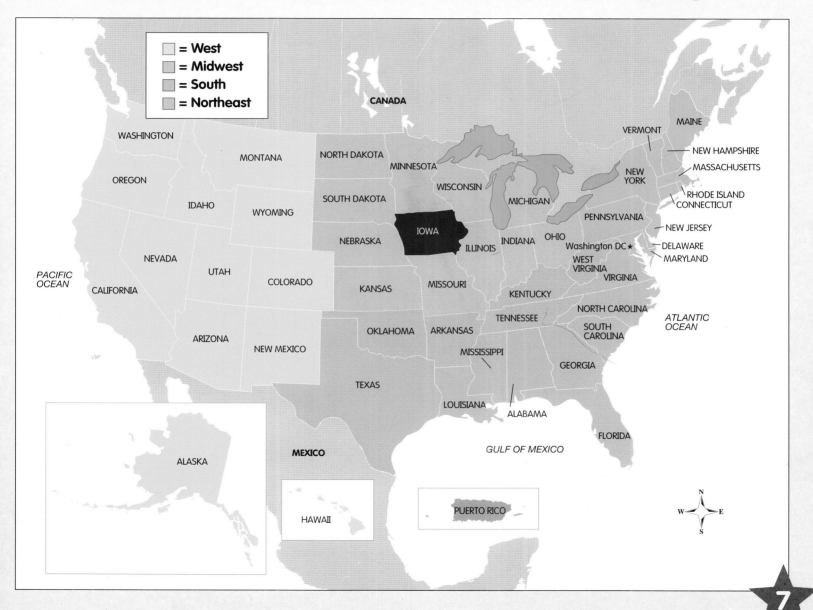

= West
= Midwest
= South
= Northeast

CANADA

WASHINGTON
MONTANA
NORTH DAKOTA
MINNESOTA
VERMONT
MAINE
NEW HAMPSHIRE
OREGON
IDAHO
WYOMING
SOUTH DAKOTA
WISCONSIN
MICHIGAN
NEW YORK
MASSACHUSETTS
RHODE ISLAND
CONNECTICUT
PENNSYLVANIA
NEW JERSEY
NEVADA
UTAH
COLORADO
NEBRASKA
IOWA
ILLINOIS
INDIANA
OHIO
Washington DC ★
DELAWARE
MARYLAND
WEST VIRGINIA
VIRGINIA
PACIFIC OCEAN
CALIFORNIA
KANSAS
MISSOURI
KENTUCKY
NORTH CAROLINA
ATLANTIC OCEAN
TENNESSEE
SOUTH CAROLINA
ARIZONA
NEW MEXICO
OKLAHOMA
ARKANSAS
MISSISSIPPI
GEORGIA
TEXAS
LOUISIANA
ALABAMA
FLORIDA

ALASKA
MEXICO
GULF OF MEXICO

HAWAII
PUERTO RICO

N
W E
S

7

IMPORTANT CITIES

Des Moines (dih-MOYN) is Iowa's **capital** and largest city. It is home to 203,433 people. The Iowa State Fair happens there every summer.

The city has many **insurance** businesses. The Meredith Corporation is also located there. It produces books, Web sites, and national magazines.

The Iowa State Capitol has five domes!

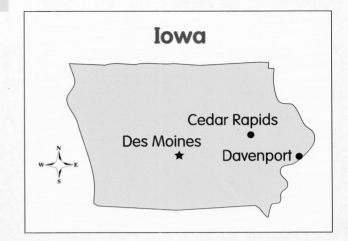

Iowa

Cedar Rapids

Des Moines

Davenport

N
W · E
S

Des Moines is located where two rivers meet.

9

The second-largest city in Iowa is Cedar Rapids. It is home to 126,326 people. It is known for having many businesses. Captain Crunch and other cereals are made in its factories.

Davenport is Iowa's third-largest city, with 99,685 people. It is on the Mississippi River. It is part of a group of cities on the Iowa and Illinois border. They are called the Quad Cities.

Cedar Rapids has many manufacturing companies.

Iowa in History

Iowa's history includes Native Americans and explorers. Native Americans have lived in the area for thousands of years. In 1673, French explorers visited the land. Later, settlers arrived.

In 1803, President Thomas Jefferson bought more land for the United States. Iowa was part of this deal known as the **Louisiana Purchase**. American explorers Meriwether Lewis and William Clark visited the new land. Iowa became a state in 1846.

Iowa was one of many places the French explored.

Timeline

1804

When Lewis and Clark visited Iowa, a group member died. In 1901, the Sergeant Floyd Monument was built in his honor.

1910

The first Drake Relays were held at Drake University. This track-and-field event still happens every year.

1800s

Iowa became the twenty-ninth state on December 28.

The first railroad to cross Iowa was built.

1846

1867

2011

Heavy snowfall caused historic flooding in Iowa in the spring. This destroyed homes and roads. Some bridges and freeways were closed for months.

1960

The Sergeant Floyd Monument in Sioux City became the first US national historic landmark.

1900s

2000s

The Keokuk Dam on the Mississippi River was finished.

The baseball movie *Field of Dreams* came out. It was filmed at the Lansing farm near Dyersville.

1913

1989

15

Across the Land

Iowa has rolling hills and flat, open land. Parts of Iowa have rich soil called loess (LEHS). The Mississippi River forms the state's eastern border. The Missouri River forms most of the western border. The state also has lakes and streams.

Many types of animals make their homes in Iowa. These include white-tailed deer, ring-necked pheasants, and bald eagles.

Did You Know?

In July, the average temperature in Iowa is 75°F (24°C). In January, it is 19°F (-7°C).

Loess is picked up and moved by wind. Over thousands of years it formed some of Iowa's cliffs and hills.

EARNING A LIVING

Iowa is a farming state. It is home to more than 90,000 farms! The state's dark, rich soil is ideal for growing crops such as corn. Iowa is also known for its dairy, cattle, and hog farming.

Education, banking, **publishing**, and **insurance** are other important businesses in Iowa. And, some people have jobs helping visitors who travel to the state.

Iowa farms produce corn, soybeans, dairy, pork, and eggs.

SPORTS PAGE

Many people think of college sports when they think of Iowa. Football, wrestling, and basketball are popular.

Several Iowa colleges are known for their exciting football and basketball games. These include Iowa State University, the University of Iowa, and the University of Northern Iowa. Drake University is known for a track-and-field event called the Drake Relays.

Did You Know?

In 1972, Iowa native Dan Gable won an Olympic gold medal in wrestling! He coached wrestling at the University of Iowa from 1972 to 1997.

Many people watch Iowa State University basketball games.

HOMETOWN HEROES

Many famous people are from Iowa. Herbert Hoover was born in West Branch in 1874. He was the thirty-first US president.

Hoover was president from 1929 to 1933. This was during a time when many people were poor and struggled to find work. Hoover and the US Congress passed laws so the government could help American businesses. But, hard times continued for many more years.

West Branch is home to the Herbert Hoover Presidential Library and Museum.

HERBERT HOOVER PRESIDENTIAL LIBRARY-MUSEUM

Hoover sent pictures of him and his dog King Tut to voters when he ran for office. Some say his dog helped him win!

John Wayne was born in Winterset in 1907. He was a top actor in Hollywood for many years.

Wayne began acting in the late 1920s. He appeared in more than 150 movies! He was best known for playing cowboy parts. He won an **Academy Award** for the 1969 film *True Grit*.

Wayne's big break was a starring part in *Stagecoach* in 1939.

Tour Book

Do you want to go to Iowa? If you visit the state, here are some places to go and things to do!

 See

Thousands of bikers cross the state in seven days during RAGBRAI. This famous event happens every July.

 Discover

The University of Iowa is famous for its Writers' Workshop. Walk on the school grounds and write a few lines.

⭐ Play

The Iowa Great Lakes area is a popular vacation spot. Swim in West Lake Okoboji's clear blue water. Or, ride a roller coaster at Arnolds Park!

⭐ Cheer

Watch the Hawkeyes play football! Their home field is Kinnick Stadium at the University of Iowa in Iowa City.

⭐ Taste

Stop in Le Mars for an ice cream cone. This small town is home to Blue Bunny Ice Cream. So, it is called "the Ice Cream Capital of the World."

A GREAT STATE

The story of Iowa is important to the United States. The people and places that make up this state offer something special to the country. Together with all the states, Iowa helps make the United States great.

In northeastern Iowa, tall hills rise above the Mississippi River.

Fast Facts

Date of Statehood:
December 28, 1846

Population (rank):
3,046,355
(30th most-populated state)

Total Area (rank):
56,273 square miles
(26th largest state)

Motto:
"Our Liberties We Prize and
Our Rights We Will Maintain"

Nickname:
Hawkeye State,
Corn State

State Capital:
Des Moines

Flag:

Flower: Wild Prairie Rose

Postal Abbreviation:
IA

Tree: Oak

Bird: Eastern Goldfinch

Important Words

Academy Award an award given by the Academy of Motion Picture Arts and Sciences to the best actors and filmmakers of the year.

capital a city where government leaders meet.

diverse made up of things that are different from each other.

insurance a contract that promises to guard people against a loss of money if something happens to them or their property.

Louisiana Purchase land the United States purchased from France in 1803. It extended from the Mississippi River to the Rocky Mountains and from Canada through the Gulf of Mexico.

publishing the business of printing the work of an author.

region a large part of a country that is different from other parts.

Web Sites

To learn more about Iowa, visit ABDO Publishing Company online. Web sites about Iowa are featured on our Book Links page. These links are routinely monitored and updated to provide the most current information available.

www.abdopublishing.com

Index